MY GRANDPA RETIRED TODAY

Library of Congress Cataloging in Publication Data

Knox-Wagner, Elaine.
My grandpa retired today.

(Concept book. Level 2)
Summary: As she helps her grandfather clean and lock up his barbershop one final time, Margey feels the pain of separation that comes with retirement almost as much as he does.
[1. Retirement—Fiction] I. Robinson, Charles, 1931- , ill. II. Title. III. Series
PZ7. K778My [E] 82-1935
ISBN 0-8075-5334-4 AACR2

Published in 1982 by Albert Whitman & Company, Niles, Illinois.
Published simultaneously in Canada by General Publishing, Limited, Toronto.
 Printed in the United States of America
Second Printing 1984

Elaine Knox-Wagner

My Grandpa Retired Today

Pictures by Charles Robinson

ALBERT WHITMAN & COMPANY, NILES, ILLINOIS

To the grandpa I didn't know but imagined;
with thanks to Margey, whose name I borrowed.

My Grandpa retired today.
I was the only kid at the party.

"Come have some cake, Margey," Grandpa said.
So I did.
We don't usually have cake at the barbershop.
It was very good. Chocolate inside and out.

Then I oiled the barber chairs and pedaled them up and down. I patted goop on my face and braids so I smelled good. I swept black hair and brown hair and a little red hair from under the counter.

Grandpa was talking and laughing with all the men.
I pulled on his sleeve.
"Should I wash the combs?" I asked.

“Toss the old papers instead,” he said.
I saluted. He saluted.
It’s an old Army game we play.

I threw the old newspapers into the barrel by the alley.
I wiped the bottoms of all the cans and bottles
and lined them straight along the shelves.
I ate a second piece of cake.

Grandpa stood in a circle of tall men.
Some I didn't even know.
I stood on a stool
and waved at him over their heads.
He waved back.
"Have some more cake," he called.

So I ate another piece of cake.
I should have washed the combs instead.
This time, the cake did not taste good.

I wiggled through the circle and took my grandpa's hand.
He smiled at me. His friends smiled at me.

My grandpa's partner slapped him on the back.
"Well, Al," he said, "time for the big surprise."

“Tata ta ta!” someone yelled.
We all turned to look.

Someone had tied a giant red bow around the barber chair with my grandpa's name on the back. And they had unbolted it from the floor.

"Since no one can take your place, Al, we decided you should take it with you," said Grandpa's partner.

Everyone clapped.
Grandpa just stared.
I got sick.

When I got back from the bathroom, the party was over.
The men were gone, the "closed" sign was in the window,
and grandpa's barber chair was driving away
in the back of a truck.

"You okay?" asked Grandpa.

I nodded. "Too much cake, I guess."

He nodded.
"Well, let's give the place
a last clean-up, then," he said.

We set out fresh towels.
We added liquids to some of the bottles.
We put the combs in the sterilizer.
We did everything we could think to do.

Finally, it was time to leave.
"Do you want to lock up?" Grandpa asked.

"You do it today," I said.

We slowly walked home,
past Finneman's Market and Sam's Floral and Riteway Cleaners.

I kicked a stone and sighed.
Grandpa kicked a stone and sighed.

We waited for a green light.
"This might be a fine summer for the beach," Grandpa said.

"I like barbershops," I said.

The light changed.
"Then again, we always did mean to get downtown
to see those dinosaur bones," he said.

"Pooh," I said. "You can see them in books."

Grandpa took my hand.
"I sure will miss the shop," he said.

"Me, too," I said.

When I went to say good night,
Grandpa was in his room, sitting in the barber chair
that said "Al" on the back.
His eyes were closed and he looked lonesome.

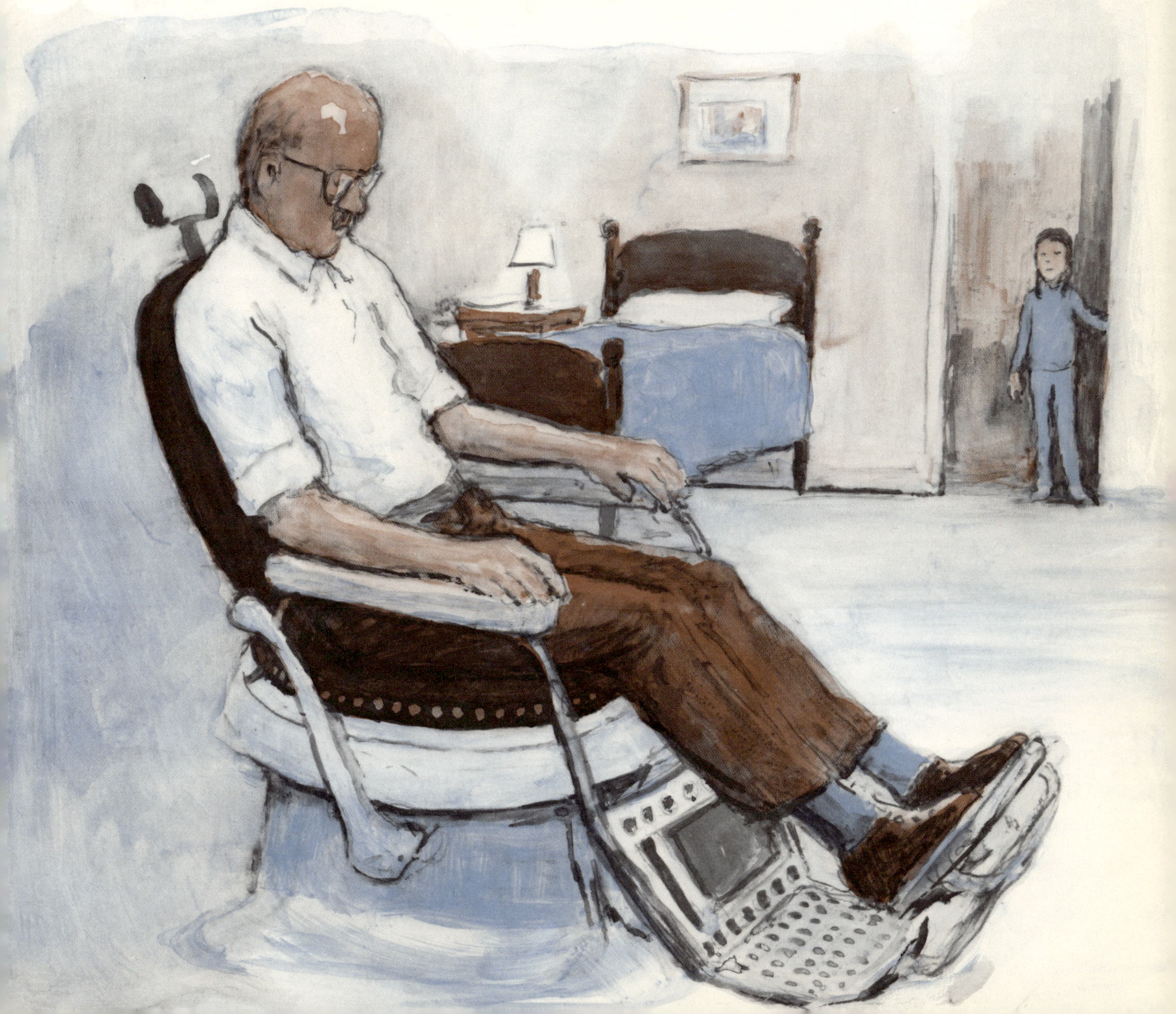

I climbed on his lap.
"There is more to life than working in a barbershop," I said.
Grandpa laughed and laughed and laughed.
So I laughed and laughed and laughed.

"I don't know where you pick up
some of the things you say," he told me.

"From you, mostly," I said.

"Off to bed with you now," he said.
"We've got things to do tomorrow."

Tomorrow,
after we fix the sticky kitchen drawers,
we'll hunt for sandals in the second-hand stores.
We'll buy paint for my chipped dresser
and eat pastrami sandwiches from the deli.

Then Grandpa and his friend who's already retired are going to teach me and my friend Joanie how to play backgammon.

Before it closes,
we'll probably go to the barbershop.
But not to stay.
Because, today, my grandpa retired.

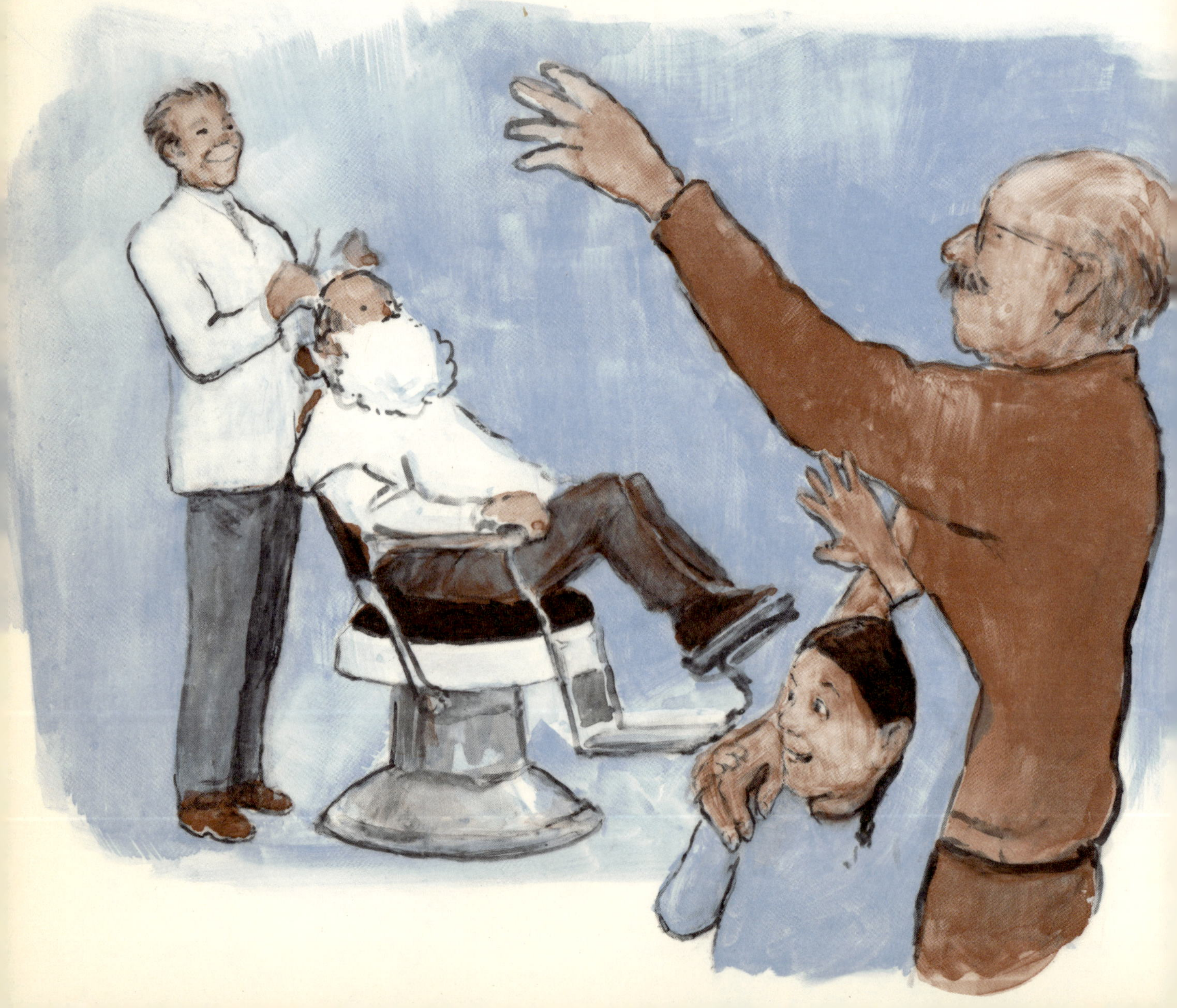